contents

Please note that Australian cup and
spoon measurements are metric.
A conversion chart appears on page 62.

smoky eggplant caviar

2 large eggplants (1kg)
⅓ cup (80ml) lemon juice
¼ cup (60ml) olive oil
1 clove garlic, crushed

1 Pierce eggplants all over with skewer or sharp knife. Cook on heated oiled grill plate (or grill or barbecue) about 30 minutes or until eggplant softens, turning every 10 minutes. Cool.
2 Halve eggplants, scoop flesh out of skin into fine strainer; discard skin. Drain 5 minutes.
3 Blend or process eggplant until pulpy; transfer to serving bowl. Stir in remaining ingredients.
4 Serve cold or at room temperature, with grissini, if desired.

makes 2 cups
preparation time 15 minutes
cooking time 30 minutes
per tablespoon 2.4g fat; 113kJ (27 cal)

vegetables with harissa and almond couscous

20g butter
1 tablespoon olive oil
2 medium brown onions (300g),
    chopped coarsely
2 cloves garlic, crushed
4cm piece fresh ginger
    (20g), grated
2 teaspoons ground cumin
2 teaspoons ground coriander
2 teaspoons finely grated
    lemon rind
1kg pumpkin, chopped coarsely
400g can chopped tomatoes
2 cups (500ml) vegetable stock
400g green beans, cut into
    5cm lengths
⅓ cup (55g) sultanas
1 tablespoon honey
¼ cup finely chopped fresh
    flat-leaf parsley
¼ cup finely chopped fresh mint
harissa and almond couscous
2 cups (500ml) vegetable stock
1 cup (250ml) water
3 cups (600g) couscous
½ cup (70g) roasted
    slivered almonds
1 tablespoon harissa

1 Heat butter and oil in large saucepan; cook onion and garlic, stirring, 5 minutes. Add ginger, spices and rind; cook about 1 minute or until fragrant. Add pumpkin, undrained tomatoes and stock; bring to a boil. Reduce heat; simmer, covered, about 15 minutes or until pumpkin is just tender.
2 Make harissa and almond couscous.
3 Add beans to tagine mixture; cook, stirring, 5 minutes. Stir sultanas, honey and chopped herbs through tagine off the heat just before serving; serve with couscous.
harissa and almond couscous Bring stock and the water to a boil in medium saucepan; remove from heat. Add couscous; cover, stand about 3 minutes or until liquid is absorbed, fluffing with fork occasionally. Use fork to gently mix almonds and harissa through couscous.

serves 6
preparation time 30 minutes
cooking time 30 minutes
per serving 14.4g fat; 2668kJ (637 cal)

vegetable couscous

1 medium kumara (400g)

1 tablespoon olive oil

60g butter

4 baby eggplants (240g),
   sliced thinly

1 large brown onion (200g),
   sliced thinly

¼ teaspoon cayenne pepper

2 teaspoons ground cumin

2 teaspoons ground coriander

1½ cups (375ml)
   vegetable stock

2 cups (400g) couscous

2 teaspoons finely grated
   lemon rind

2 cups (500ml) boiling water

410g can chickpeas,
   rinsed, drained

2 tablespoons lemon juice

100g baby spinach leaves

¼ cup loosely packed fresh
   flat-leaf parsley leaves

1 Chop kumara into 1cm cubes. Heat oil and half the butter in large frying pan; cook kumara with eggplant and onion, stirring, until vegetables brown. Add spices; cook about 2 minutes or until fragrant. Stir in stock; bring to a boil. Reduce heat; simmer, uncovered, about 15 minutes or until vegetables are just tender.

2 Meanwhile, combine couscous in large heatproof bowl with rind, the water and half the remaining butter. Cover; stand about 5 minutes or until liquid is absorbed, fluffing occasionally with fork.

3 Add chickpeas and remaining butter to vegetable mixture; cook, stirring, until butter melts. Stir in couscous, juice, spinach and parsley.

serves 4
preparation time 20 minutes
cooking time 25 minutes
per serving 20.1g fat; 3246kJ (775 cal)
tips Remove vegetable mixture from heat, then immediately add couscous, spinach and parsley; the greens will wilt in the heat of the vegetables.
serving suggestion Serve with a bowl of cumin-scented yogurt and warm fresh pitta.

moroccan lamb shanks
with polenta and white beans

1½ cups (300g) dried
 haricot beans
12 french-trimmed lamb
 shanks (3kg)
¼ cup (35g) plain flour
1 tablespoon olive oil
2 medium red onions (340g),
 chopped finely
2 cloves garlic, crushed
2 teaspoons ground cumin
½ teaspoon ground cardamom
½ teaspoon ground ginger
2 teaspoons finely grated
 lemon rind
⅓ cup (80ml) lemon juice
2 x 400g cans
 crushed tomatoes
2½ cups (625ml) beef stock
¼ cup (70g) tomato paste
3 cups (750ml) water
3 cups (750ml) milk
2 cups (340g) polenta
2 teaspoons finely grated
 lemon rind, extra
¼ cup finely chopped fresh
 flat-leaf parsley
¼ cup finely chopped
 fresh coriander

1 Cover beans with cold water in large bowl.
Stand overnight; drain.

2 Coat lamb in flour; shake off excess. Heat oil
in large saucepan; cook lamb, in batches, until
browned all over. Add onion and garlic; cook,
stirring, until onion is soft. Add spices to pan;
cook, stirring, about 2 minutes or until fragrant.

3 Stir in beans, rind, juice, undrained tomatoes,
stock and paste; bring to a boil. Reduce heat;
simmer, covered, 40 minutes. Uncover;
simmer about 50 minutes or until lamb and
beans are tender.

4 Heat the water and milk in large saucepan
(do not boil). Add polenta; cook, stirring, about
5 minutes or until liquid is absorbed and
polenta softens.

5 Serve lamb mixture on polenta; sprinkle with
combined extra rind, parsley and coriander.

serves 6
preparation time 25 minutes
(plus standing time)
cooking time 2 hours
per serving 15.1g fat; 3114kJ (744 cal)
tip You can use any dried bean (navy, cannellini,
great northern or even chickpeas) in this recipe.

moroccan chicken and chickpea soup

2 tablespoons olive oil
340g chicken breast fillets
1 large brown onion (200g),
   chopped finely
2 cloves garlic, crushed
4 cm piece fresh ginger
   (20g), grated
1½ teaspoons ground cumin
1½ teaspoons ground
   coriander
1 teaspoon ground turmeric
½ teaspoon sweet paprika
1 cinnamon stick
¼ cup (35g) plain flour
1 litre (4 cups) chicken stock
1 litre (4 cups) water
2 x 300g cans chickpeas,
   rinsed, drained
2 x 400g cans
   crushed tomatoes
2 tablespoons finely chopped
   preserved lemon
1 tablespoon coarsely
   chopped fresh coriander

1 Heat half the oil in large frying pan; cook chicken, uncovered, about 10 minutes or until browned and cooked through. Drain chicken on absorbent paper, cool 10 minutes; using two forks, shred chicken coarsely.

2 Heat remaining oil in large saucepan; cook onion, garlic and ginger, stirring, until onion softens. Add cumin, ground coriander, turmeric, paprika and cinnamon; cook, stirring, until fragrant.

3 Add flour; cook, stirring, until mixture bubbles and thickens. Gradually stir in stock and the water; cook, stirring, until mixture comes to a boil. Simmer, uncovered, 20 minutes.

4 Add chickpeas and undrained tomatoes, bring to a boil. Reduce heat: simmer, uncovered, 10 minutes.

5 Add chicken and lemon to soup; stir over heat until soup is hot. Just before serving, stir in fresh coriander.

serves 6
preparation time 20 minutes
cooking time 50 minutes
per serving 11.3g fat; 1205kJ (288 cal)

harira

This hearty lamb and vegetable soup from Morocco is traditionally eaten during the four weeks of Ramadan, after sundown, to break the day's fast.

½ cup (100g) dried chickpeas
500g boned lamb shoulder
2 tablespoons olive oil
1 large brown onion (200g),
    chopped coarsely
2 teaspoons ground ginger
1 tablespoon ground cumin
1 teaspoon ground cinnamon
2 teaspoons ground coriander
6 saffron threads
3 trimmed celery stalks (300g),
    chopped coarsely
7 medium tomatoes (1kg),
    seeded, chopped coarsely
2.5 litres (10 cups) water
½ cup (100g) brown lentils
¼ cup coarsely chopped
    fresh coriander

1 Place chickpeas in small bowl, cover with water; stand overnight, drain.
2 Trim lamb of excess fat; cut into 2cm cubes.
3 Heat oil in large saucepan; cook onion, stirring, until soft. Add spices; cook, stirring, about 2 minutes or until fragrant. Add lamb and celery; cook, stirring, about 2 minutes or until lamb is coated in spice mixture. Add tomato; cook, stirring, about 10 minutes or until tomato softens slightly. Stir in the water and drained chickpeas; bring to a boil. Reduce heat; simmer, covered, about 1½ hours or until lamb is tender, stirring occasionally.
4 Stir in lentils; cook, covered, about 30 minutes or until lentils are just tender.
5 Just before serving, stir coriander into soup.

serves 6
preparation time 20 minutes
(plus standing time)
cooking time 2 hours 10 minutes
per serving 15.6g fat; 1317kJ (314 cal)
tips Drained canned chickpeas can be substituted for dried chickpeas.
Two 400g cans of crushed tomatoes can be substituted for fresh tomatoes.
serving suggestion Serve with lemon wedges and toasted pide.

lamb and vegetable stew

2 tablespoons olive oil
2 medium red onions (340g), chopped coarsely
1½ teaspoons ground ginger
½ teaspoon ground cinnamon
2 x 400g cans crushed tomatoes
1.5 litres (6 cups) vegetable stock
pinch saffron threads
1kg diced lamb
1 cup (200g) white long-grain rice
1 cup (200g) red lentils
2 x 400g cans chickpeas, rinsed, drained
1kg frozen broad beans, thawed, peeled
½ cup coarsely chopped fresh coriander leaves
½ cup coarsely chopped fresh flat-leaf parsley

1   Heat oil in large heavy-based saucepan; cook onion, ginger and cinnamon, stirring, until onion is soft.
2   Add undrained tomatoes, stock, saffron and lamb; bring to a boil. Simmer, covered, about 1½ hours or until lamb is tender.
3   Add rice and lentils; simmer, uncovered, about 20 minutes or until rice and lentils are just tender. Add chickpeas and beans; simmer, uncovered, until hot. Just before serving, stir through coriander and parsley.

serves 8
preparation time 10 minutes
cooking time 2 hours 10 minutes
per serving 18.4g fat; 2253kJ (538 cal)
tip Use fresh broad beans, if in season.

couscous cakes with mediterranean vegetables

1½ tablespoons olive oil
1 medium red onion (170g),
  sliced thickly
3 baby eggplant (180g),
  sliced thickly
2 medium green zucchini
  (240g), chopped coarsely
250g cherry tomatoes
250g yellow teardrop
  tomatoes
¼ cup (60ml) balsamic vinegar
1 clove garlic, crushed
1½ cups (300g) couscous
1½ cups (375ml) boiling water
¼ cup (20g) finely grated
  parmesan cheese
2 tablespoons coarsely
  chopped fresh basil
60g butter

1 Heat 2 teaspoons of the oil in large frying pan; cook onion, eggplant and zucchini, stirring, until vegetables soften.

2 Stir in tomatoes, vinegar, garlic and remaining oil; cook, stirring occasionally, about 10 minutes or until tomatoes are very soft.

3 Meanwhile, combine couscous with the water in large heatproof bowl; cover, stand 5 minutes or until liquid is absorbed, fluffing with fork occasionally. Stir in cheese and basil.

4 Heat half the butter in large frying pan, press half the couscous mixture into four egg rings in pan; cook until browned lightly on both sides. Carefully remove egg rings, then couscous cakes. Repeat using remaining butter and couscous mixture.

5 Serve vegetables with couscous cakes.

serves 4
preparation time 15 minutes
cooking time 20 minutes
per serving 21.7g fat; 2153kJ (514 cal)

pumpkin tagine with date couscous

2 tablespoons olive oil
1 large brown onion (200g),
   sliced thickly
3 cloves garlic, crushed
½ teaspoon ground chilli
½ teaspoon ground turmeric
1 teaspoon ground cinnamon
1 teaspoon ground coriander
1 teaspoon ground cumin
3 cups (750ml)
   vegetable stock
5 cups (800g) coarsely
   chopped pumpkin
1 cup (150g) frozen broad
   beans, thawed, peeled
1 tablespoon brown sugar
¾ cup (100g) coarsely
   chopped seeded dates
2 tablespoons coarsely
   chopped fresh coriander
date couscous
50g butter, chopped coarsely
2 cups (200g) couscous
2 cups (500ml) boiling water
½ cup (70g) coarsely chopped
   seeded dates
⅓ cup coarsely chopped
   fresh coriander

1 Heat oil in medium saucepan. Add onion, garlic and spices; cook, stirring, 3 minutes or until fragrant.
2 Add stock and pumpkin, bring to a boil; reduce heat, simmer, covered, about 10 minutes or until pumpkin is almost tender.
3 Uncover; simmer 5 minutes or until pumpkin mixture thickens slightly.
4 Meanwhile, make date couscous.
5 Add remaining ingredients to pumpkin mixture; cook, stirring, until heated through.
6 Serve pumpkin tagine with couscous.
date couscous Combine butter, couscous and the water in large heatproof bowl, cover; stand about 5 minutes or until liquid is absorbed, fluffing with fork occasionally. Stir in dates and coriander.

serves 4
preparation time 15 minutes
cooking time 20 minutes
per serving 21.8g fat; 2861kJ (684)
tip You need to buy a piece of pumpkin weighing about 1kg to make this dish.

moroccan lamb with couscous

8 lamb fillets (800g)
1 tablespoon ground cumin
1 tablespoon ground coriander
1 teaspoon ground cinnamon
¾ cup (210g) low-fat yogurt
1½ cups (300g) couscous
1½ cups (375ml) boiling water
1 teaspoon peanut oil
⅓ cup (55g) dried currants
2 teaspoons finely grated lemon rind
2 teaspoons lemon juice
¼ cup coarsely chopped fresh coriander leaves

1 Combine lamb, spices and ⅓ cup of the yogurt in medium bowl, cover; refrigerate 3 hours or overnight.
2 Cook lamb on heated oiled grill plate (or grill or barbecue) until browned and cooked as desired. Cover; stand 5 minutes then slice thinly.
3 Meanwhile, combine couscous, the water and oil in large heatproof bowl, cover; stand 5 minutes or until liquid is absorbed, fluffing with fork occasionally. Stir in currants, rind, juice and fresh coriander; toss with fork to combine.
4 Serve lamb with couscous; drizzle with remaining yogurt.

serves 4
preparation time 15 minutes (plus refrigeration time)
cooking time 15 minutes
per serving 9.3g fat; 2193kJ (524 cal)
tip Substitute some finely chopped preserved lemon for the lemon juice and rind in the couscous.

spicy couscous chicken with fresh corn salsa

Couscous, the North African cereal made from semolina, lends an intriguing crunch to the coating on the chicken.

½ teaspoon ground cumin
¼ teaspoon ground coriander
¼ teaspoon garam masala
¼ teaspoon ground turmeric
1 cup (250ml) chicken stock
1 cup (200g) couscous
700g chicken breast fillets
1 egg white, beaten lightly
2 trimmed corn cobs (500g)
2 medium tomatoes (300g),
    seeded, chopped coarsely
1 small avocado (200g),
    chopped coarsely
2 tablespoons red wine vinegar
4 green onions,
    chopped finely

1 Preheat oven to 220°C/200°C fan-forced.
2 Place spices in medium saucepan; cook, stirring, over medium heat, until fragrant; add stock. Bring to a boil; stir in couscous. Remove from heat; stand, covered, about 5 minutes or until liquid is absorbed, fluffing with fork occasionally.
3 Coat chicken with egg white then with couscous. Place chicken in large lightly oiled baking dish; bake, uncovered, about 10 minutes or until chicken is cooked through. Cover to keep warm.
4 Meanwhile, remove kernels from corn cobs. Cook kernels in small pan of boiling water, uncovered, about 2 minutes or until just tender; drain. Rinse under cold water; drain. Combine corn with remaining ingredients in medium bowl. Serve corn salsa with thickly sliced chicken.

serves 4
preparation time 15 minutes
cooking time 12 minutes
per serving 19.1g fat; 2515kJ (600 cal)

chicken tagine with olives and preserved lemon

In Morocco, the word "tagine" refers both to a slowly cooked stew and the special cone-topped pottery casserole dish in which it is served.

1 tablespoon olive oil
1 tablespoon butter
8 chicken thigh cutlets (1.5kg), skin removed
1 large red onion (300g), chopped finely
½ teaspoon saffron threads, roasted, crushed
1 teaspoon ground cinnamon
1 teaspoon ground ginger
1½ cups (375ml) chicken stock
16 seeded large green olives
2 tablespoons finely chopped preserved lemon

1 Heat oil and butter in large heavy-based saucepan with tight-fitting lid; cook chicken, in batches, until browned all over.

2 Place onion and spices in same pan; cook, stirring, until onion softens. Return chicken to pan with stock; bring to a boil. Reduce heat; simmer, covered, about 30 minutes or until chicken is cooked through.

3 Remove chicken from pan; cover to keep warm. Skim and discard fat from top of pan liquid; bring to a boil. Reduce heat; cook, stirring, until liquid reduces by half.

4 Return chicken to pan with olives and lemon; stir until heated through. Serve tagine with couscous, if desired.

serves 4
preparation time 15 minutes
cooking time 45 minutes
per serving 25.9g fat; 1831kJ (437)
tip Saffron threads should be roasted in a small dry frying pan over medium heat until just fragrant, then crushed with the back of a spoon.

spicy roasted pumpkin couscous

1 tablespoon olive oil
2 cloves garlic, crushed
1 large red onion (300g), sliced thickly
500g pumpkin, peeled, chopped coarsely
3 teaspoons ground cumin
2 teaspoons ground coriander
1 cup (200g) couscous
1 cup (250ml) boiling water
20g butter
2 tablespoons coarsely chopped fresh flat-leaf parsley

1 Preheat oven to 220°C/200°C fan-forced.
2 Heat oil in medium flameproof baking dish; cook garlic, onion and pumpkin, stirring, until vegetables are browned lightly. Add spices; cook, stirring, about 2 minutes or until fragrant.
3 Place baking dish in oven; roast pumpkin mixture, uncovered, about 15 minutes or until pumpkin is just tender.
4 Meanwhile, combine couscous with the water and butter in large heatproof bowl; cover, stand about 5 minutes or until liquid is absorbed, fluffing with fork occasionally. Stir in parsley.
5 Toss pumpkin mixture through couscous.

serves 4
preparation time 10 minutes
cooking time 30 minutes
per serving 9.8g fat; 1361kJ (325 cal)

kofta with fresh green onion couscous

Soak 12 bamboo skewers in cold water for at least one hour before use to prevent scorching and splintering.

1kg mince
1 medium brown onion (150g), chopped finely
2 cloves garlic, crushed
2 tablespoons lemon juice
1½ teaspoons ground cumin
1½ teaspoons ground coriander
¼ cup (40g) roasted pine nuts
2 tablespoons finely chopped fresh mint
1 tablespoon finely chopped fresh coriander
1 egg
2 cups (500ml) beef stock
2 cups (400g) couscous
30g butter, chopped
2 green onions, sliced thinly

1 Combine mince, brown onion, garlic, juice, spices, nuts, herbs and egg in large bowl. Roll heaped tablespoons of mixture into balls; thread three balls on each skewer. Place kofta skewers on tray, cover; refrigerate 30 minutes.
2 Place stock in medium saucepan; bring to a boil. Remove from heat, add couscous and butter, cover; stand about 5 minutes or until liquid is absorbed, fluffing with fork occasionally.
3 Meanwhile, cook kofta on heated oiled grill plate (or grill or barbecue) until browned all over and cooked through.
4 Toss green onion with couscous; serve with kofta, accompanied by a bowl of combined yogurt and chopped cucumber, if desired.

serves 4
preparation time 20 minutes
(plus refrigeration time)
cooking time 15 minutes
per serving 42.7g fat; 4114kJ (983 cal)

veal cutlets with couscous salad

8 veal cutlets (1.5kg)
⅓ cup (80ml) balsamic vinegar
⅓ cup (80ml) olive oil
1 clove garlic, crushed
1½ cups (375ml) beef stock
1½ cups (300g) couscous
150g fetta cheese, cut into 2cm pieces
⅔ cup (120g) seeded kalamata olives
1 medium red capsicum (200g), chopped coarsely
¼ cup coarsely chopped fresh mint
¼ cup (60ml) lemon juice
⅓ cup (80ml) olive oil, extra
1 clove garlic, crushed

1 Combine cutlets in large bowl with vinegar, oil and garlic; toss to coat cutlets all over in marinade. Cover; refrigerate 20 minutes.

2 Meanwhile, bring stock to a boil in medium saucepan. Remove from heat; stir in couscous. Cover; stand about 5 minutes or until liquid is absorbed, fluffing with fork occasionally. Add remaining ingredients; toss gently to combine.

3 Drain cutlets; discard marinade. Cook cutlets on heated oiled grill plate (or grill or barbecue) until browned both sides and cooked as desired. Serve couscous salad with cutlets.

serves 4
preparation time 10 minutes (plus refrigeration time)
cooking time 10 minutes
per serving 50.8g fat; 4094kJ (978 cal)

moroccan beef with citrus couscous

2 cloves garlic, crushed
1 teaspoon ground ginger
1 tablespoon ground cumin
2 teaspoons ground coriander
500g piece beef butt fillet
1 tablespoon harissa paste
1 cup (250ml) beef stock
200g seeded green olives,
    crushed lightly
½ cup coarsely chopped
    fresh coriander

citrus couscous

2 medium oranges (480g)
1 cup (250ml) water
1 cup (250ml) orange juice
2 cups (400g) couscous
¼ cup (35g) roasted
    slivered almonds
1 tablespoon thinly sliced
    preserved lemon
1 small red onion (100g),
    sliced thinly
500g red radishes,
    trimmed, sliced thinly

1 Combine garlic and spices in medium bowl; reserve about a third of the spice mixture. Add beef to bowl with remaining spice mixture; toss to coat beef all over. Cook beef on heated oiled grill plate (or grill or barbecue) until charred lightly both sides and cooked as desired. Cover; stand 10 minutes then slice thickly.

2 Meanwhile, make citrus couscous.

3 Cook harissa and remaining spice mixture in dry heated small frying pan until fragrant. Add stock; bring to a boil. Reduce heat; simmer, uncovered, about 3 minutes or until harissa dressing reduces by half. Remove from heat; stir in olives and coriander.

4 Serve beef on citrus couscous; drizzle with warm harissa dressing.

citrus couscous Remove skin and white pith from oranges; cut in half, slice thinly. Place the water and juice in medium saucepan; bring to a boil. Remove from heat; stir in couscous. Cover; stand about 5 minutes or until liquid is absorbed, fluffing with fork occasionally. Add orange and remaining ingredients; toss gently to combine.

serves 4
preparation time 15 minutes
cooking time 20 minutes
per serving 15.5g fat; 3114kJ (744 cal)
tip Butt fillet is fillet from the rump; rump steak can be substituted, if preferred.

moroccan blue-eye fillets with fruity couscous

1 clove garlic, crushed
1cm piece fresh ginger (5g), grated
1 teaspoon ground cumin
½ teaspoon ground turmeric
½ teaspoon hot paprika
½ teaspoon ground coriander
4 x 200g blue-eye fillets, skin removed
1 tablespoon olive oil
fruity couscous
2 cups (400g) couscous
2 cups (500ml) boiling water
50g butter
1 large pear (330g), chopped finely
½ cup (80g) finely chopped dried apricots
½ cup (100g) coarsely chopped dried figs
½ cup coarsely chopped fresh flat-leaf parsley
¼ cup (40g) roasted pine nuts

1 Combine garlic, ginger and spices in large bowl. Add fish; toss to coat fish in spice mixture. Heat oil in large frying pan; cook fish, in batches, until browned both sides and cooked as desired.
2 Meanwhile, make fruity couscous.
3 Divide couscous among serving plates; top with fish. Accompany with a bowl of combined yogurt and coarsely chopped fresh coriander, if desired.
fruity couscous Combine couscous, the water and butter in large heatproof bowl, cover; stand about 5 minutes or until liquid is absorbed, fluffing with fork occasionally. Stir in remaining ingredients.

serves 4
preparation time 20 minutes
cooking time 15 minutes
per serving 27.5g fat; 3816kJ (912 cal)

merguez and couscous salad

*A small, spicy sausage – believed to have originated in Tunisia but eaten throughout
North Africa and Spain – merguez is traditionally made with lamb meat and is easily
identified by its chilli-red colour. It can be fried, grilled or roasted, and can be found
in many butchers, delicatessens and sausage specialty stores.*

500g merguez sausages
1½ cups (375ml) beef stock
1½ cups (300g) couscous
20g butter
1 tablespoon finely grated lemon rind
¾ cup coarsely chopped fresh flat-leaf parsley
120g baby rocket leaves
⅓ cup (50g) roasted pine nuts
2 fresh small red thai chillies, sliced thinly
1 small red onion (100g), sliced thinly
1 clove garlic, crushed
⅓ cup (80ml) lemon juice
2 tablespoons olive oil

1 Cook sausages on heated grill plate (or grill or barbecue) until browned
and cooked through. Drain on absorbent paper; slice thickly.
2 Meanwhile, bring stock to a boil in medium saucepan. Remove from
heat; stir in couscous and butter. Cover; stand about 10 minutes or until
liquid is absorbed, fluffing with fork occasionally.
3 Place sausage and couscous in large bowl with remaining ingredients;
toss gently to combine.

serves 4
preparation time 15 minutes
cooking time 10 minutes
per serving 45g fat; 3621kJ (865 cal)

vegetable tagine with olive and parsley couscous

1 tablespoon olive oil
1 medium red onion (170g),
    sliced thinly
2 cloves garlic, crushed
1 teaspoon dried chilli flakes
1 teaspoon ground coriander
½ teaspoon ground turmeric
1 teaspoon cumin seeds
500g pumpkin,
    chopped coarsely
2 medium potatoes (400g),
    chopped coarsely
2½ cups (625ml)
    vegetable stock
300g can chickpeas,
    rinsed, drained
½ cup coarsely chopped
    fresh coriander
olive and parsley couscous
1½ cups (375ml)
    vegetable stock
1½ cups (300g) couscous
30g butter
1⅓ cups (200g) seeded
    kalamata olives
½ cup coarsely chopped
    fresh flat-leaf parsley

1 Heat oil in medium saucepan; cook onion, garlic and chilli, stirring, until onion softens. Add spices and seeds; cook, stirring, until mixture is fragrant. Add pumpkin and potato; stir to coat vegetables in spice mixture.
2 Stir in stock; bring to a boil. Reduce heat; simmer, uncovered, about 10 minutes or until vegetables are almost tender. Stir in chickpeas; simmer, uncovered, about 10 minutes or until vegetables are tender.
3 Meanwhile, make olive and parsley couscous.
4 Stir coriander into tagine. Serve couscous topped with vegetable tagine.
olive and parsley couscous Bring stock to a boil in medium saucepan. Remove from heat; stir in couscous and butter. Cover; stand about 5 minutes or until liquid is absorbed, fluffing with fork occasionally. Stir in olives and parsley.

serves 4
preparation time 20 minutes
cooking time 20 minutes
per serving 14.4g fat; 2541kJ (607 cal)
tip You need a piece of pumpkin weighing approximately 600g for this recipe.

chicken, preserved lemon and green bean salad

You need to purchase a large barbecued chicken for this recipe.

1 cup (160g) sultanas
1 cup (250ml) warm water
¼ cup (60ml) lemon juice
1 barbecued chicken (900g)
175g baby green beans, trimmed
2 tablespoons finely chopped preserved lemon rind
340g jar marinated quartered artichokes, drained
2 cups firmly packed fresh flat-leaf parsley leaves
2 tablespoons olive oil
2 tablespoons white wine vinegar

1 Combine sultanas, the water and juice in medium bowl, cover; stand 5 minutes. Drain; discard liquid.
2 Meanwhile, discard skin and bones from chicken; slice meat thickly.
3 Boil, steam or microwave beans until tender; drain. Rinse under cold water; drain.
4 Place sultanas, chicken and beans in large bowl with remaining ingredients; toss gently to combine.

serves 4
preparation time 15 minutes
cooking time 5 minutes
per serving 20.2g fat; 1998kJ (477 cal)

lemon-fetta couscous
with steamed vegetables

You need about half a butternut pumpkin for this recipe.

600g butternut pumpkin, chopped coarsely
2 small green zucchini (180g), chopped coarsely
2 small yellow zucchini (180g), chopped coarsely
300g spinach, trimmed, chopped coarsely
2 cups (500ml) vegetable stock
2 cups (400g) couscous
¼ cup (60ml) lemon juice
⅓ cup coarsely chopped fresh basil
200g low-fat fetta cheese, chopped coarsely
¼ cup finely chopped preserved lemon rind
6 green onions, sliced thinly

1 Boil, steam or microwave pumpkin, zucchinis and spinach, separately, until tender; drain.
2 Meanwhile, bring stock to a boil in large saucepan. Add couscous, remove from heat, cover; stand about 5 minutes or until liquid is absorbed, fluffing with fork occasionally. Place couscous and vegetables in large bowl with remaining ingredients; toss gently to combine.

serves 4
preparation time 20 minutes
cooking time 10 minutes
per serving 9.4g fat; 2427kJ (581 cal)

warm lamb tabbouleh

500g lamb eye of loin, sliced thinly
2 cloves garlic, crushed
¼ cup (60ml) lemon juice
2 tablespoons olive oil
1 cup (160g) burghul
250g cherry tomatoes, halved
8 green onions, chopped thinly
¼ cup (60ml) lemon juice, extra
½ cup coarsely chopped fresh flat-leaf parsley
½ cup coarsely chopped fresh mint

1 Combine lamb, garlic, juice and half the oil in large bowl, cover; refrigerate 3 hours or overnight.
2 Cover burghul with cold water in small bowl; stand 15 minutes, drain. Rinse burghul under cold water; drain, squeeze out excess moisture.
3 Heat remaining oil in wok; stir-fry lamb mixture, in batches, until browned. Cover to keep warm.
4 Stir-fry burghul, tomato and onion in wok until onion is browned lightly.
5 Toss extra juice, parsley and mint through tabbouleh off the heat; serve with lamb mixture.

serves 4
preparation time 10 minutes (plus refrigeration and standing time)
cooking time 25 minutes
per serving 21.1g fat; 1852kJ (443 cal)

citrus chicken with chickpea salad

4 chicken breast fillets (800g), halved
1 tablespoon finely grated lemon rind
1 tablespoon finely grated lime rind
300g can chickpeas, rinsed, drained
1 medium red onion (170g), chopped finely
2 medium tomatoes (300g), chopped coarsely
1 tablespoon finely chopped fresh coriander leaves
1 medium avocado (250g), chopped coarsely
1 tablespoon lemon juice

1 Combine chicken and rinds in medium bowl, cover; refrigerate 3 hours.
2 Combine chickpeas, onion, tomato, coriander, avocado and juice in medium bowl; mix well.
3 Cook chicken on heated oiled grill plate (or grill or barbecue) until chicken is browned both sides and cooked through. Spoon chickpea salad into serving bowls; top with warm chicken.

serves 4
preparation time 20 minutes (plus refrigeration time)
cooking time 20 minutes
per serving 14.9g fat; 1480kJ (353 cal)

moroccan beef salad with couscous

1 cup (250ml) vegetable stock
1½ cups (300g) couscous
500g beef rump steak
½ cup (75g) dried apricots, sliced
½ cup (80g) sultanas
1 medium red onion (170g), sliced thinly
¼ cup finely chopped fresh mint
2 tablespoons finely chopped fresh dill
1 tablespoon pine nuts
2 teaspoons cumin seeds
¾ cup (180ml) oil-free french dressing

1 Cook beef on heated oiled grill plate (or grill or barbecue) until browned both sides and cooked as desired. Cover, stand 5 minutes then slice thinly.

2 Meanwhile, bring stock to a boil in large pan, remove from heat; add couscous. Cover, stand about 5 minutes or until liquid is absorbed, fluffing with fork occasionally. Add apricots, sultanas, onion and herbs to couscous; mix gently.

3 Place pine nuts and cumin in dry small frying pan; stir over low heat until seeds are just fragrant and pine nuts are roasted. Combine seeds and nuts with dressing in small bowl; drizzle over beef and couscous.

serves 4
preparation time 15 minutes
cooking time 15 minutes
per serving 14.2g fat; 2495kJ (596 cal)

spiced apricot and chicken tagine

1 tablespoon olive oil
1kg chicken thigh fillets, chopped coarsely
2 cloves garlic, crushed
1 large brown onion (200g), chopped finely
¼ teaspoon ground cinnamon
½ teaspoon ground cumin
½ teaspoon ground ginger
½ teaspoon ground turmeric
1 cup (250ml) hot chicken stock
1 tablespoon honey
1 cup (150g) dried apricots
1 tablespoon cornflour
1 tablespoon water
½ cup (80g) blanched almonds
2 tablespoons coarsely chopped fresh coriander

1 Combine oil, chicken, garlic, onion and spices in large microwave-safe bowl; cook, covered, on MEDIUM-HIGH (70%) 15 minutes, stirring once during cooking.
2 Add stock, honey and apricots; cook, uncovered, on MEDIUM-HIGH (70%) about 5 minutes or until apricots are tender. Stir in blended cornflour and the water; cook, uncovered, on MEDIUM-HIGH (70%) about 3 minutes or until mixture boils and thickens slightly, stirring once during cooking.
3 Cook nuts on microwave-safe plate, uncovered, on HIGH (100%) about 3 minutes or until browned lightly, stirring twice during cooking. Stir nuts and coriander into tagine; serve with couscous (see recipe, page 52), if desired.

serves 4
preparation time 25 minutes
cooking time 30 minutes
per serving 26.8g fat; 2450kJ (585 cal)

lamb hot pot with couscous

600g lamb leg chops
1 tablespoon plain flour
2 teaspoons olive oil
1 medium brown onion (150g), cut into thin wedges
1 teaspoon ground cinnamon
1 teaspoon ground turmeric
1 cup water (250ml)
½ cup beef stock (125ml)
100g prunes, seeded
2 tablespoons finely chopped fresh coriander
couscous
1 cup (250ml) boiling water
1 cup (200g) couscous

1 Trim all visible fat from lamb. Cut lamb into cubes; toss in flour.

2 Heat oil in large saucepan; cook onion until soft. Add lamb; cook until lamb is browned all over. Stir in cinnamon and turmeric; cook 1 minute.

3 Stir in the water, stock and prunes; bring to a boil. Reduce heat; simmer, covered, about 30 minutes or until lamb is tender.

4 Meanwhile, make couscous.

5 Serve lamb with couscous; sprinkle with coriander.

couscous Combine the water and couscous in medium bowl; stand 5 minutes or until liquid is absorbed, fluffing with fork occasionally.

serves 2
preparation time 15 minutes
cooking time 45 minutes
per serving 20.3g fat; 3648kJ (871 cal)

pitta salad rolls with lamb kebabs

500g diced lamb
¼ cup (60ml) lemon juice
1 clove garlic, crushed
⅓ cup (80ml) olive oil
8 pitta pocket breads
80g baby spinach leaves
2 medium tomatoes (300g), sliced thickly
½ cup (60g) seeded black olives, quartered
200g fetta cheese, crumbled

1 Combine lamb, juice, garlic and 2 tablespoons of the oil in large bowl. Cover; refrigerate 3 hours or overnight. Remove lamb from marinade; reserve marinade.
2 Thread lamb onto eight skewers. Heat reserved marinade and remaining oil in large frying pan; cook kebabs, turning, until lamb is cooked as desired.
3 Serve kebabs on pitta bread accompanied with spinach, tomato, olives and cheese.

serves 4
preparation time 25 minutes (plus refrigeration time)
cooking time 10 minutes
per serving 39.5g fat; 3140kJ (750 cal)
tip You need to soak eight bamboo skewers in water for at least an hour before using to stop them from splintering and scorching during cooking.

merguez, beetroot and lentil salad

Golden beetroots have a slightly sweeter flavour than the red variety, and can be found at most greengrocers. When trimming the beetroots, leave a little of the stalk intact to prevent bleeding during cooking.

2 cups (400g) brown lentils
2 sprigs fresh thyme
20 baby red beetroots (500g)
20 baby golden beetroots (500g)
8 merguez sausages (640g)
1 large brown onion (200g),
  chopped finely
2 teaspoons yellow
  mustard seeds
2 teaspoons ground cumin
1 teaspoon ground coriander
½ cup (125ml) chicken stock
300g spinach, trimmed,
  chopped coarsely
thyme dressing
1 teaspoon finely chopped
  fresh thyme
1 clove garlic, crushed
½ cup (125ml) red wine
  vinegar
¼ cup (60ml) extra virgin
  olive oil

1 Make thyme dressing.
2 Cook lentils with thyme sprigs, uncovered, in large saucepan of boiling water until tender; drain lentils, discard thyme sprigs. Place lentils in large bowl with half the dressing; toss gently to combine.
3 Meanwhile, discard leaves and most of the stalk from each beetroot. Boil, steam or microwave unpeeled beetroots until just tender; drain. When cool enough to handle, peel beetroots then cut in half.
4 Cook sausages in heated large oiled frying pan until browned and cooked through. Cool 5 minutes; slice thickly.
5 Reheat pan; cook onion, seeds, cumin and coriander, stirring, until onion softens. Add stock; bring to a boil. Remove from heat; stir in spinach.
6 Add spinach mixture, beetroot, sausage and remaining dressing to lentil mixture; toss gently to combine.
thyme dressing Combine ingredients in screw-top jar; shake well.

serves 4
preparation time 30 minutes
cooking time 50 minutes
per serving 45.2g fat; 3968kJ (948 cal)

lamb and apricot tagine
with orange and lemon couscous

1⅔ cups (250g) dried apricots
¾ cup (180ml) orange juice
½ cup (125ml) boiling water
2 tablespoons olive oil
900g diced lamb
2 medium red capsicums
 (400g), chopped coarsely
1 large brown onion (200g),
 chopped coarsely
2 medium kumara (800g),
 chopped coarsely
3 cloves garlic, crushed
1 teaspoon ground cinnamon
2 teaspoons ground cumin
2 teaspoons ground
 coriander
1 cup (250ml) dry red wine
1 litre (4 cups) chicken stock
2 tablespoons honey
1 cup loosely packed fresh
 coriander leaves
¾ cup (200g) low-fat yogurt
orange and lemon couscous
1 litre (4 cups) water
4 cups (800g) couscous
1 tablespoon finely grated
 orange rind
2 teaspoons finely grated
 lemon rind
2 teaspoons finely grated
 lime rind

1 Combine apricots, juice and the water in small bowl. Cover; stand 45 minutes.
2 Meanwhile, heat half the oil in large saucepan; cook lamb, in batches, until browned all over.
3 Heat remaining oil in same pan; cook capsicum, onion, kumara, garlic and ground spices, stirring, until onion softens and mixture is fragrant. Add wine, bring to a boil; simmer, uncovered, about 5 minutes or until liquid reduces by half.
4 Return lamb to pan with undrained apricots, stock and honey; bring to a boil. Reduce heat, simmer, covered, about 50 minutes or until lamb is tender. Remove from heat; stir in fresh coriander.
5 Make orange and lemon couscous.
6 Serve lamb and apricot tagine on couscous; drizzle with yogurt.
orange and lemon couscous Bring the water to a boil in medium saucepan; stir in couscous and rinds. Remove from heat; stand, covered, about 5 minutes or until liquid is absorbed, fluffing with fork occasionally.

serves 8
preparation time 20 minutes
(plus standing time)
cooking time 1 hour
per serving 12.8g fat;1837kJ (439 cal)

glossary

basil an aromatic herb; there are many types, but the most commonly used is sweet, or common, basil.

beans

broad also known as fava, windsor and horse beans; are available dried, fresh, canned and frozen. Fresh and frozen, they are best peeled twice (discarding both the outer long green pod and the beige-green tough inner shell).

cannellini small, dried white bean similar in appearance and flavour to great northern, navy or haricot bean.

beetroot also known as red beets; round root vegetable.

blue-eye fillets also known as trevally, deep sea trevalla or blue-eye cod; thick, moist white-fleshed fish fillets.

burghul also known as bulghur wheat; hulled, steamed wheat kernels that, once dried, are crushed into various-sized grains.

butter use salted or unsalted (sweet) butter; 125g is equal to one stick of butter.

butternut pumpkin used interchangeably with the word squash; is pear-shaped with orange skin and flesh.

capsicum also known as bell pepper or, simply, pepper. Discard seeds and membranes before use.

cardamom has an aromatic, sweetly rich flavour; available in pod, seed or ground form.

cayenne pepper an extremely hot, dried red chilli, usually purchased ground; both arbol and guajillo chillies are the fresh sources for cayenne.

cheese

fetta Greek in origin; a crumbly-textured goat or sheep-milk cheese with a sharp, salty taste.

parmesan also known as parmigiano; a hard, grainy cow-milk cheese.

chickpeas also called garbanzos, hummus or channa; an irregularly round sandy-coloured legume.

chilli use rubber gloves when seeding and chopping fresh chillies as they can burn your skin. Removing seeds and membranes lessens the heat level.

flakes, dried deep-red, dehydrated chilli slices and whole seeds.

red thai small, medium hot, and bright red in colour.

cinnamon dried inner bark of the shoots of the cinnamon tree; available in stick or ground form.

coriander also known as cilantro or chinese parsley; bright-green leafy herb with a pungent flavour. Also sold as seeds, whole or ground. The stems and roots of coriander are also used in Thai cooking. Coriander seeds are no substitute for fresh coriander.

cornflour also known as cornstarch; used as a thickening agent in cooking.

couscous a fine, grain-like cereal product, made from semolina.

cumin also known as zeera or comino; has a spicy, nutty flavour. Available in seed form or dried and ground.

currants, dried tiny, almost black, raisins.

dates fruit of the date palm tree, eaten fresh or dried. Oval, plump and thin-skinned, with a honey-sweet flavour and sticky texture.

eggplant also known as aubergine. Ranging in size from tiny to very large, and in colour from pale-green to deep-purple.

flour plain an all-purpose flour, made from wheat.

french-trimmed sometimes just seen as "frenched"; all excess sinew, gristle and fat from the bone end of meat cutlets, racks or shanks are removed and the bones scraped clean.

garam masala a blend of spices based on varying proportions of cardamom, cinnamon, cloves, coriander, fennel and cumin, roasted and ground together.

ginger also known as green or root ginger; a thick gnarled root of a tropical plant.

ground also known as powdered ginger; cannot be substituted for fresh ginger.

harissa a paste made from dried red chillies, garlic, oil and caraway seeds; is a staple of Moroccan cooking.

kalamata olives small, sharp-tasting, brine-cured black olives.

kumara Polynesian name of orange-fleshed sweet potato often confused with yam.

lentils dried pulses often identified by and named after their colour.

merguez a small, spicy sausage traditionally made with lamb meat and is easily identified by its chilli-red colour. Available from butchers, delicatessens and sausage specialty stores.

mince meat also known as ground meat, as in beef, pork, lamb, chicken and veal.

mustard seeds, yellow mild seeds, available from most major supermarkets and health food shops.

oil
olive made from ripened olives. *Extra virgin* and *virgin* are the best, while *extra light* or *light* refers to taste, not fat levels.

peanut pressed ground nuts; has a high smoke point (the capacity to handle high heat without burning).

vegetable any of a number of oils sourced from plants rather than animal fats.

onion
brown and white are interchangeable.

green also known as scallion or, incorrectly, shallot; an immature onion picked before the bulb has formed, having a long, bright-green edible stalk.

red also known as spanish, red spanish or bermuda onion; a sweet-flavoured, large, purple-red onion.

paprika ground dried red capsicum (bell pepper), available sweet or hot.

parsley, flat-leaf also known as continental parsley or italian parsley.

pine nut also known as pignoli; not in fact a nut but a small, cream-coloured kernel from pine cones.

pitta a wheat-flour pocket bread also known as lebanese bread. Is sold in large, flat pieces that separate into two thin rounds or small thick pieces called *pocket pitta*.

polenta also known as cornmeal; a flour-like cereal made of dried corn (maize). Also the name of the dish made from it.

preserved lemon lemons bottled in salt and oil for several months. Rinse the lemons well then remove and discard flesh, using the rind only.

prawns also called shrimp.

radish a peppery vegetable related to the mustard plant. The small round red variety is the mildest.

rocket also known as arugula, rugula and rucola; a peppery-tasting green leaf. *Baby rocket leaves* are both smaller and less peppery.

saffron available in strands or ground form; imparts a yellow-orange colour to food once infused.

spinach also known as english spinach and, incorrectly, silver beet.

stock available in cans, bottles or tetra packs or as cubes or powder.

sultanas dried grapes also known as golden raisins.

tomatoes
cherry small, round tomatoes also known as tiny tim or tom thumb.
yellow teardrop small yellow pear-shaped tomatoes.

turmeric a rhizome related to galangal and ginger; must be grated or pounded to release its somewhat acrid aroma and pungent flavour.

vinegar
balsamic originally from Modena, Italy, there are now many balsamic vinegars on the market ranging in pungency and quality depending on how long they have been aged; use the most expensive sparingly.
red wine based on fermented red wine.
white wine made from white wine.

zucchini also known as courgette.

conversion chart

MEASURES

One Australian metric measuring cup holds approximately 250ml, one Australian metric tablespoon holds 20ml, one Australian metric teaspoon holds 5ml.

The difference between one country's measuring cups and another's is within a 2- or 3-teaspoon variance, and will not affect your cooking results. North America, New Zealand and the United Kingdom use a 15ml tablespoon. All cup and spoon measurements are level. The most accurate way of measuring dry ingredients is to weigh them. When measuring liquids, use a clear glass or plastic jug with metric markings.

We use large eggs with an average weight of 60g.

DRY MEASURES

METRIC	IMPERIAL
15g	½oz
30g	1oz
60g	2oz
90g	3oz
125g	4oz (¼lb)
155g	5oz
185g	6oz
220g	7oz
250g	8oz (½lb)
280g	9oz
315g	10oz
345g	11oz
375g	12oz (¾lb)
410g	13oz
440g	14oz
470g	15oz
500g	16oz (1lb)
750g	24oz (1½lb)
1kg	32oz (2lb)

LIQUID MEASURES

METRIC	IMPERIAL
30ml	1 fluid oz
60ml	2 fluid oz
100ml	3 fluid oz
125ml	4 fluid oz
150ml	5 fluid oz (¼ pint/1 gill)
190ml	6 fluid oz
250ml	8 fluid oz
300ml	10 fluid oz (½ pint)
500ml	16 fluid oz
600ml	20 fluid oz (1 pint)
1000ml (1 litre)	1¾ pints

LENGTH MEASURES

METRIC	IMPERIAL
3mm	⅛in
6mm	¼in
1cm	½in
2cm	¾in
2.5cm	1in
5cm	2in
6cm	2½in
8cm	3in
10cm	4in
13cm	5in
15cm	6in
18cm	7in
20cm	8in
23cm	9in
25cm	10in
28cm	11in
30cm	12in (1ft)

OVEN TEMPERATURES

These oven temperatures are only a guide for conventional ovens.
For fan-forced ovens, check the manufacturer's manual.

	°C (CELSIUS)	°F (FAHRENHEIT)	GAS MARK
Very slow	120	250	½
Slow	150	275 – 300	1 – 2
Moderately slow	160	325	3
Moderate	180	350 – 375	4 – 5
Moderately hot	200	400	6
Hot	220	425 – 450	7 – 8
Very hot	240	475	9

index

Are you missing some of the world's favourite cookbooks?

The Australian Women's Weekly cookbooks are available from bookshops, cookshops, supermarkets and other stores all over the world. You can also buy direct from the publisher, using the order form below.

MINI SERIES £3.50 190x138MM 64 PAGES

TITLE	QTY	TITLE	QTY	TITLE	QTY
4 Fast Ingredients		Grills & Barbecues		Roast	
4 Kids 2 Cook		Healthy Everyday Food 4 Kids		Salads	
15-minute Feasts		Ice-creams & Sorbets		Simple Slices	
50 Fast Chicken Fillets		Indian Cooking		Simply Seafood	
50 Fast Desserts		Italian Favourites		Soup plus	
Barbecue Chicken		Indonesian Favourites		Spanish Favourites	
Biscuits, Brownies & Bisottti		Jams & Jellies		Stir-fries	
Bites		Japanese Favourites		Stir-fry Favourites	
Bowl Food		Kebabs & Skewers		Summer Salads	
Burgers, Rösti & Fritters		Kids Party Food		Tagines & Couscous	
Cafe Cakes		Lebanese Cooking		Tapas, Antipasto & Mezze	
Cafe Food		Low-Fat Delicious		Tarts	
Casseroles & Curries		Low Fat Fast		Tex-Mex	
Char-grills & Barbecues		Malaysian Favourites		Thai Favourites	
Cheesecakes, Pavlova & Trifles		Mince Favourites		The Fast Egg	
Chinese Favourites		Microwave		The Young Chef	
Chocolate Cakes		Muffins		Vegetarian	
Crumbles & Bakes		Noodles & Stir-fries		Vegie Main Meals	
Cupcakes & Cookies		Old-Fashioned Desserts		Vietnamese Favourites	
Dips & Dippers		Outdoor Eating		Wok	
Dried Fruit & Nuts		Packed Lunch			
Drinks		Party Food			
Easy Pies & Pastries		Pickles and Chutneys			
Fast Fillets		Pasta			
Fishcakes & Crispybakes		Potatoes			
Gluten-free Cooking		Quick Desserts		TOTAL COST	£

Photocopy and complete coupon below

Name _____

Address _____

_____ Postcode _____

Country _____ Phone (business hours) _____

Email*(optional) _____

* By including your email address, you consent to receipt of any email regarding this magazine, and other emails which inform you of ACP's other publications, products, services and events, and to promote third party goods and services you may be interested in.

I enclose my cheque/money order for £ _____ or please charge £ _____ to my:

☐ Access ☐ Mastercard ☐ Visa ☐ Diners Club

Card number [| | | | | | | | | | | | | | | |]

3 digit security code *(found on reverse of card)* _____

Cardholder's signature _____ Expiry date ____ /__

To order: Mail or fax – photocopy or complete the order form above, and send your credit card details or cheque payable to: Australian Consolidated Press (UK), 10 Scirocco Close, Moulton Park Office Village, Northampton NN3 6AP, phone (+44) (01) 604 642200, fax (+44) (01) 604 642300, e-mail books@acpuk.com or order online at www.acpuk.com

Non-UK residents: We accept the credit cards listed on the coupon, or cheques, drafts or International Money Orders payable in sterling and drawn on a UK bank. Credit card charges are at the exchange rate current at the time of payment. All pricing current at time of going to press and subject to change/availability.

Postage and packing UK: Add £1.00 per order plus 75p per book.

Postage and packing overseas: Add £2.00 per order plus £1.50 per book. **Offer ends 31.12.2008**